Bingo was a small black and white puppy.

He had two bright eyes, a big wet nose and a very waggly tail.

One day Bingo was looking for somewhere to play.

'I will play in here,'
said Bingo.

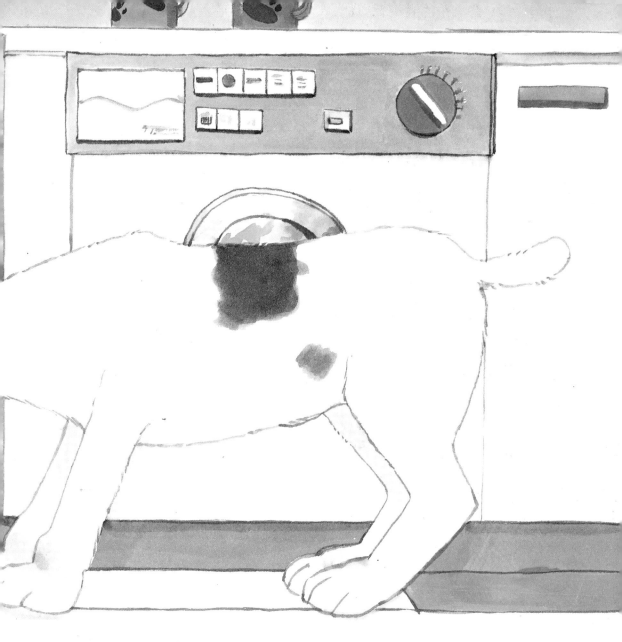

'No, you will not!'
said Mum.

'I will play in here,'
said Bingo.

'No, you will not!'
said Mum.

'Can I play in here?'
said Bingo.

'No, no, no!' said Mum.

'But you can play here,' said Mum.